The Human Body: Organs and Functions

GALLBLADDER

Priyanka Das

LIGHTBOX
openlightbox.com

LIGHTBOX

Go to
www.openlightbox.com
and enter this book's
unique code.

ACCESS CODE

LBXV2925

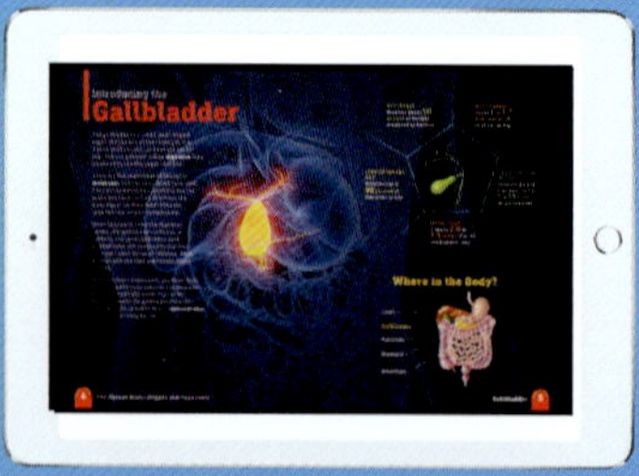

Lightbox is an all-inclusive digital solution for the teaching and learning of curriculum topics in an original, groundbreaking way. Lightbox is based on National Curriculum Standards.

LIGHTBOX SUPPLEMENTARY RESOURCES

SHARE
Share titles within your Learning Management System (LMS) or Library Circulation System

CURRICULUM
Find national and state curriculum correlations

CITATION
Create bibliographical references following APA, CMOS, and MLA styles

STANDARD FEATURES OF LIGHTBOX

AUDIO High-quality narration using text-to-speech system

ACTIVITIES Printable PDFs that can be emailed and graded

SLIDESHOWS Pictorial overviews of key concepts

VIDEOS Embedded high-definition video clips

WEBLINKS Curated links to external, child-safe resources

TRANSPARENCIES Step-by-step layering of maps, diagrams, charts, and timelines

INTERACTIVE MAPS Interactive maps and aerial satellite imagery

QUIZZES Ten multiple-choice questions that are automatically graded and emailed for teacher assessment

KEY WORDS Matching key concepts to their definitions

This title is part of our Lightbox digital subscription

Lightbox Grades 6–8 Subscription
ISBN 978-1-5105-6068-0

Access hundreds of Lightbox titles with our digital subscription. Sign up for a **FREE** subscription trial at **www.openlightbox.com/trial**

The digital components of this book are guaranteed to stay active for at least five years from the date of publication.

The Human Body: Organs and Functions

GALLBLADDER

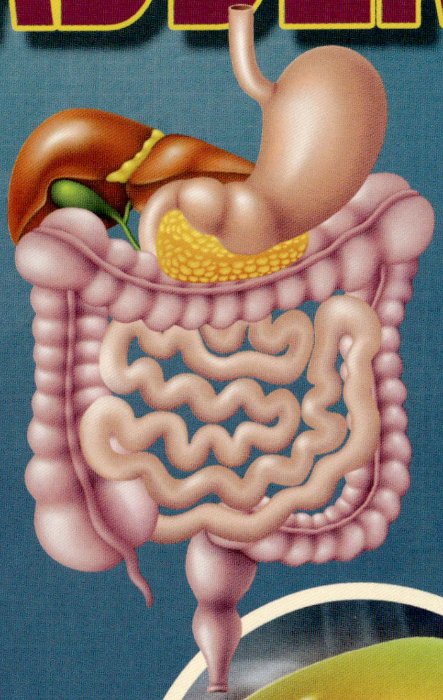

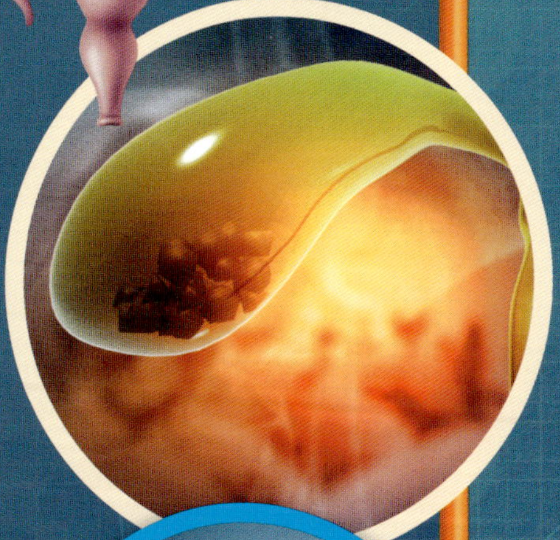

CONTENTS

Introducing the
Gallbladder

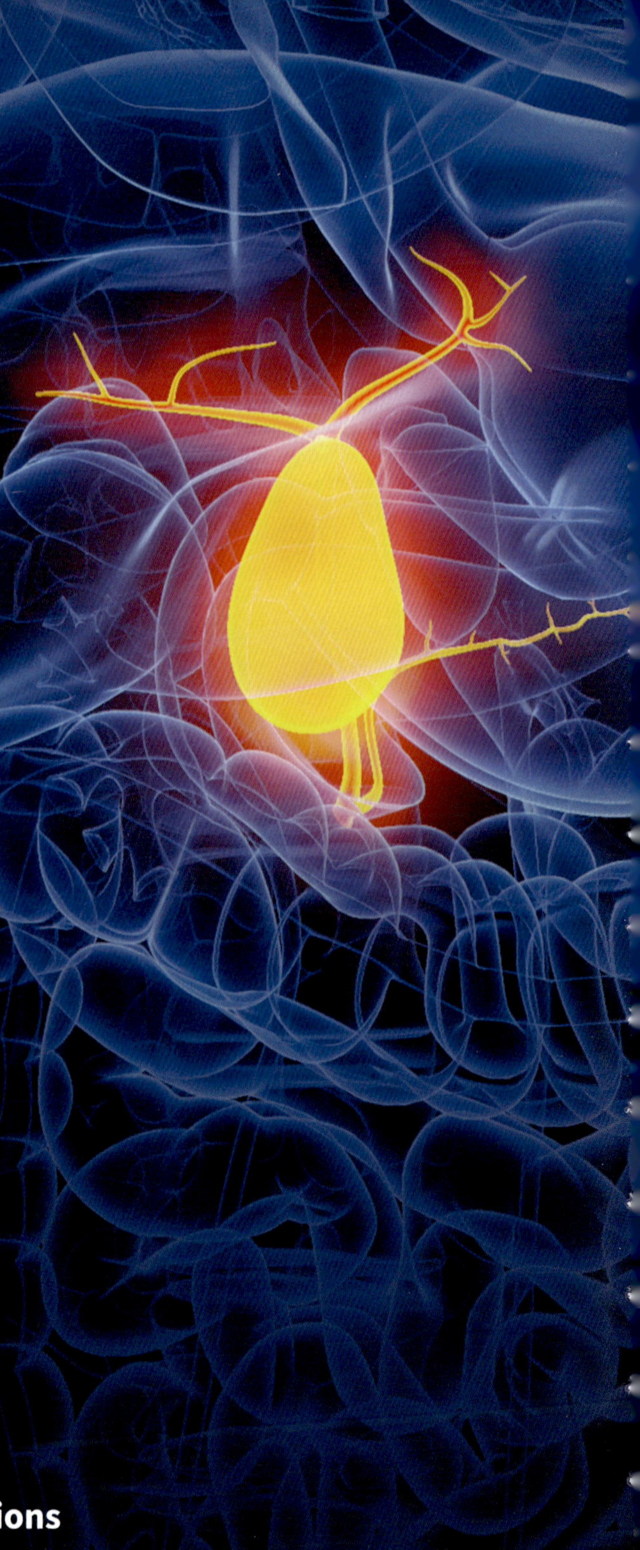

The gallbladder is a small, pear-shaped **organ**. Also known as the cholecyst, it is hollow and functions as a storage sac for bile. This is a greenish-yellow **digestive** fluid produced by another organ, the liver.

There are four main types of biological **molecules** that the body needs from food. These are carbohydrates, proteins, nucleic acids, and lipids, or fats. Bile helps the body digest fats. It breaks large fats into smaller components.

When fatty foods enter the digestive system, the gallbladder contracts, or tightens. This sends bile into a duct, or small tube. Bile ducts carry bile into an organ called the small intestine. Here, it mixes with food and breaks down the fats contained in the food.

While the liver continuously produces bile, the gallbladder only releases it in response to meals, especially those high in fats. Between meals, the gallbladder remains relaxed. The organ fills up with bile and **concentrates** it so that it is ready for use.

BILE INTAKE
Receives about **50 percent** of the bile produced by the liver

BILE STORAGE
Stores **1** to **2.7 fluid ounces** (30 to 80 milliliters) of bile

CONCENTRATING BILE
Removes up to **90 percent** of the water in bile

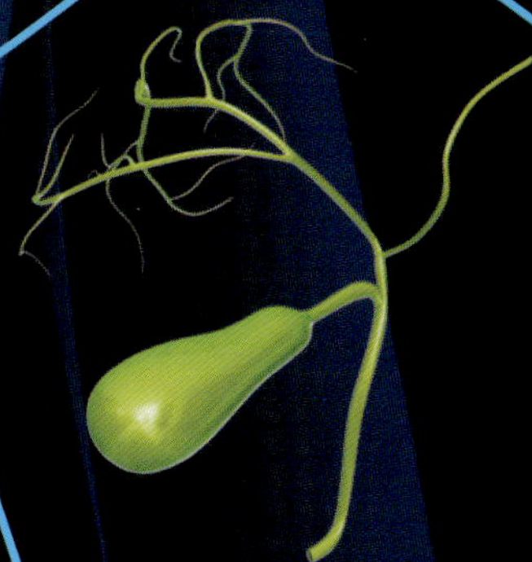

CONCENTRATION FACTOR
Thickens the bile it receives so it is **5** to **18 times** as concentrated

SIZING IT UP
About **2.8** to **3.9 inches** (7 to 10 centimeters) long

Where in the Body?

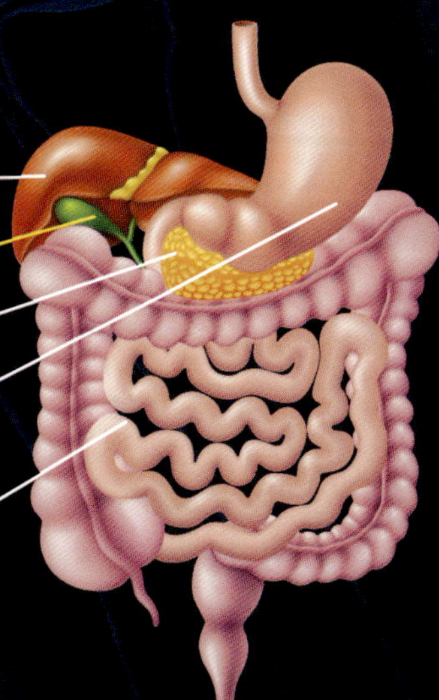

The Body's Organ Systems

The human body is made up of 11 main organ systems that keep the body healthy and functioning. Each system includes organs that perform related tasks. The gallbladder is part of the digestive system. It works with other digestive organs to help the body break down and absorb **nutrients** from food.

Most of the organs in the digestive system are part of the gastrointestinal (GI) tract. Food travels through this tract, which begins at the mouth, continues through the esophagus, stomach, and intestines, and ends with the anus. The digestive system also includes the liver, pancreas, and gallbladder. These accessory organs release fluids that help break down food. The fluids travel through ducts and enter the small intestine.

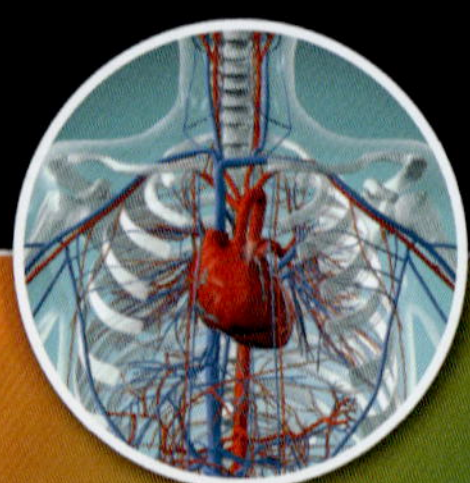

Circulatory System
Transports blood, moving substances to and from the body's **cells**

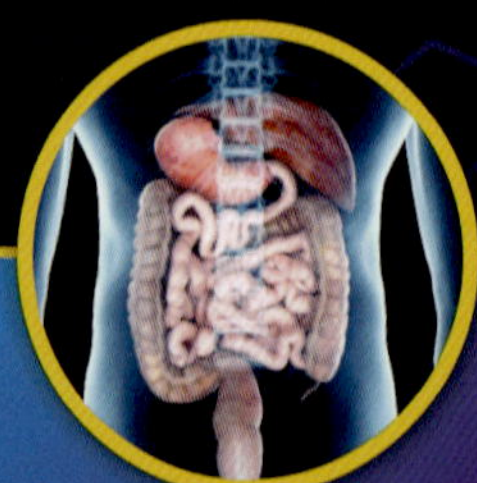

Digestive System
Extracts energy and nutrients from food

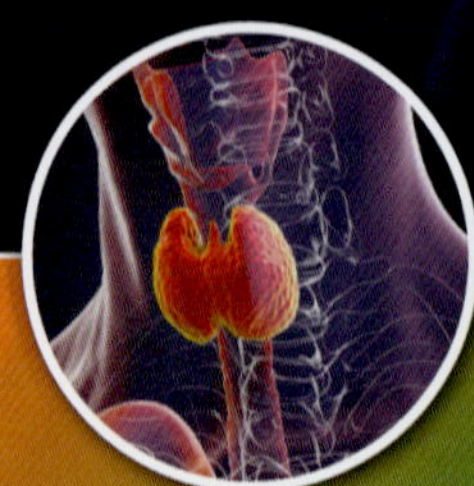

Endocrine System
Controls the release of **hormones** and maintains **homeostasis**

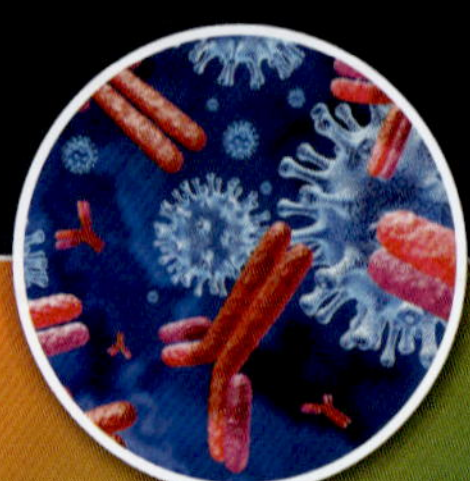

Immune System
Protects the body from attack by **pathogens**

Integumentary System
Protects the internal organs and is primarily made up of skin

Muscular System
Works together with the skeletal system to allow the body to move

The digestive system has a close connection with the circulatory system. Once food is broken down in the stomach and intestines, its nutrients enter the blood. This blood travels to the liver first. The liver processes the nutrients and removes harmful substances. Then, the blood transports the nutrients to the rest of the body.

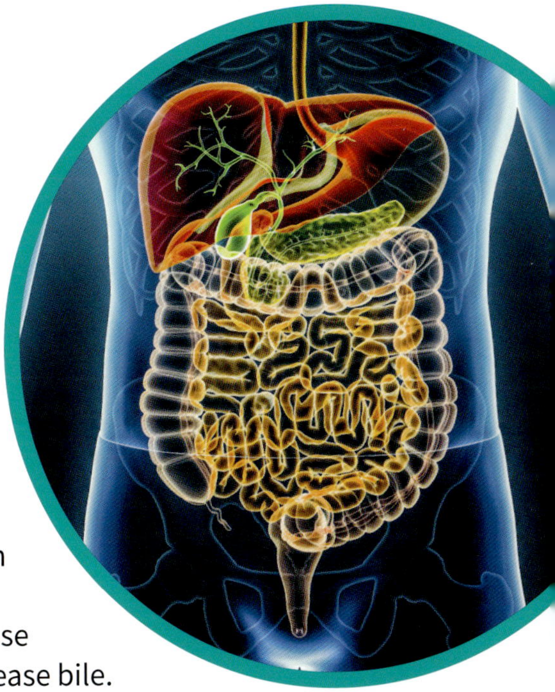

Many digestive system organs release or respond to endocrine system hormones. When foods high in fats and proteins enter the small intestine, the organ releases a hormone called cholecystokinin (CCK). This hormone sends signals to the pancreas to release **enzymes** and to the gallbladder to contract and release bile.

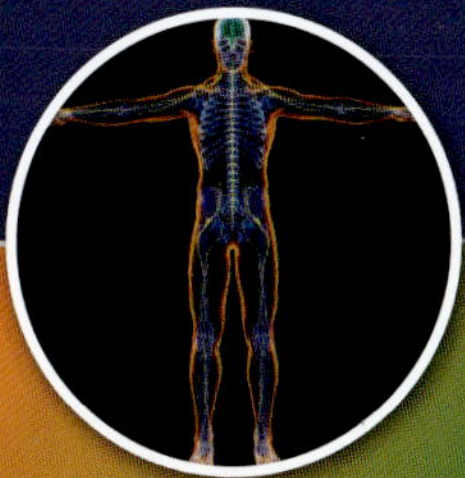

Nervous System
Carries signals between the brain and the rest of the body

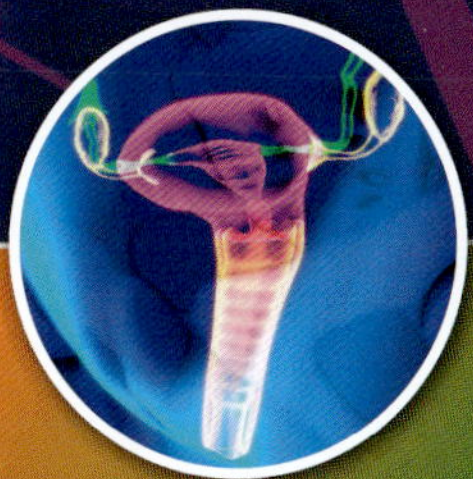

Reproductive System
Enables people to have children

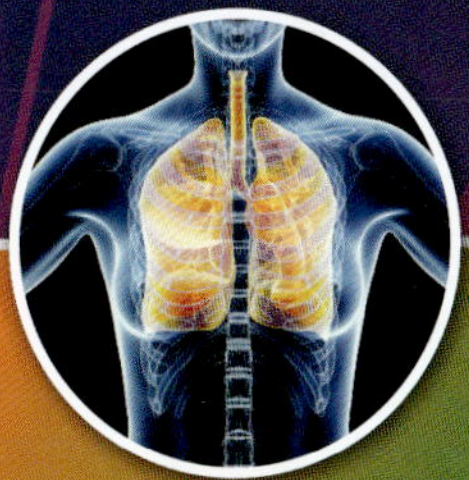

Respiratory System
Removes carbon dioxide from the body and takes in oxygen

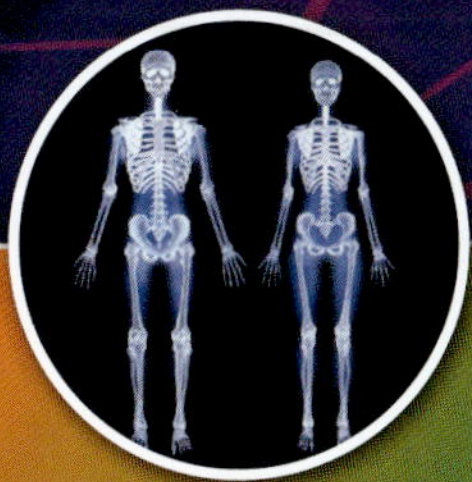

Skeletal System
Supports the body and protects the internal organs

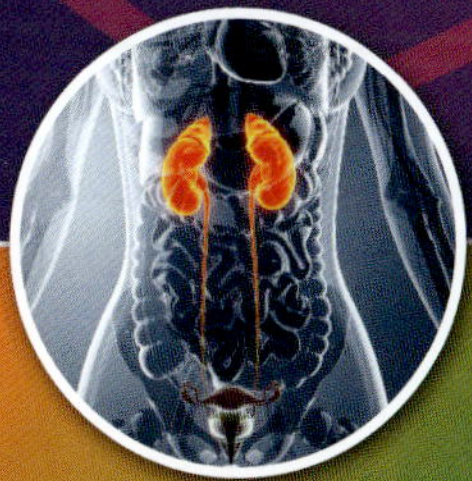

Urinary System
Filters blood, removing excess water and some waste products

Structure of the Gallbladder

The gallbladder is in the right side of the upper **abdominal cavity** and located directly beneath the liver. Its three main sections are the neck, body, and fundus. The neck is narrow and connects to the cystic duct, which carries bile in and out of the gallbladder. In the middle is the body, the largest section. Farthest away from the bile ducts is the fundus, the rounded base.

Three main layers make up the wall of the gallbladder. The innermost layer is called the mucosa. It has many folds that allow the gallbladder to expand as it fills with bile. The middle layer is made of **smooth muscle**. When CCK is released after a meal, this muscle layer contracts to push bile out. The outermost layer is the serosa. It covers and protects the gallbladder.

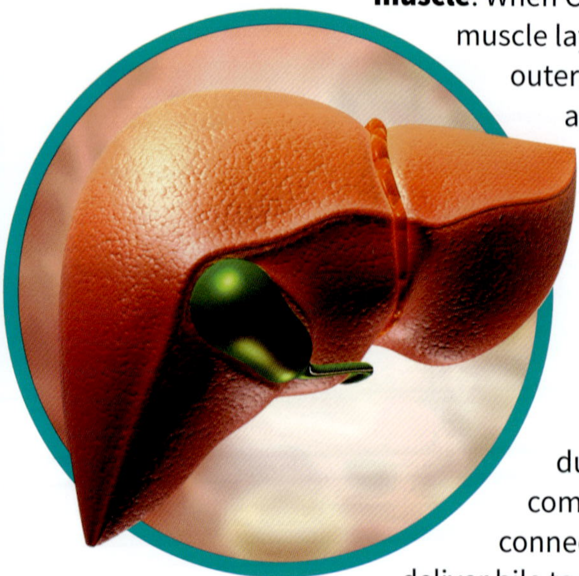

Bile ducts connect the gallbladder to both the liver and the uppermost part of the small intestine, called the duodenum. Bile produced in the liver is carried away by the left and right **hepatic** ducts. They join to form the common hepatic duct, which connects to the cystic duct to deliver bile to the gallbladder. Bile exits the gallbladder through the cystic duct. This duct joins with the common hepatic duct to form the common bile duct.

Together, the liver, gallbladder, and bile ducts form a structure called the biliary tract, or biliary tree. The pancreas is also connected to the common bile duct through the pancreatic duct. These two ducts join together to empty their contents into the duodenum.

Biliary Tree

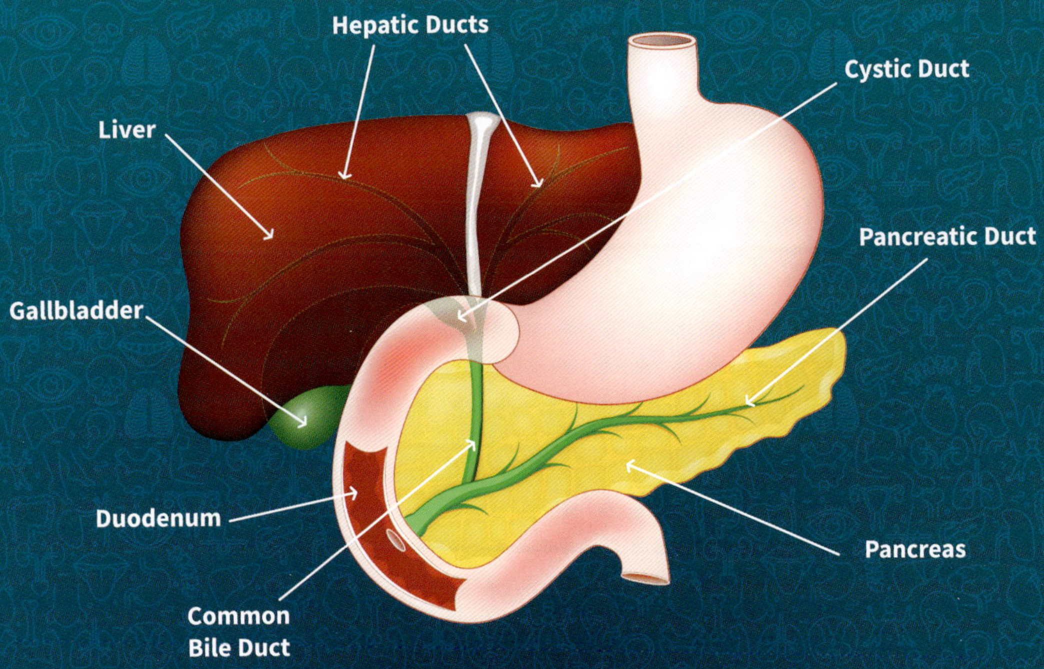

Gallbladder Anatomy

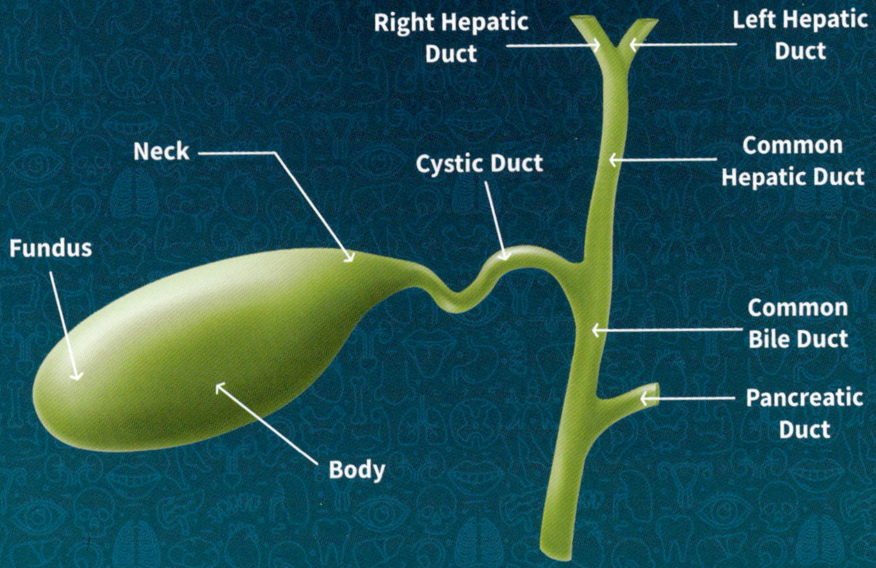

Role in the Body

By storing, concentrating, and releasing bile, the gallbladder plays a key role in digestion. Bile contains water, bile salts, and waste products, among other substances. In addition to its primary role as a digestive fluid, bile helps the liver remove toxins and waste products from the body.

Receiving Bile

Liver cells called hepatocytes use water, bile salts, a fat called cholesterol, bile **pigments**, toxins, and waste products to produce bile. When bile flows away from the liver through the hepatic ducts, some of it continues through the common bile duct and enters the small intestine right away. Half or more, however, travels through the cystic duct to the gallbladder.

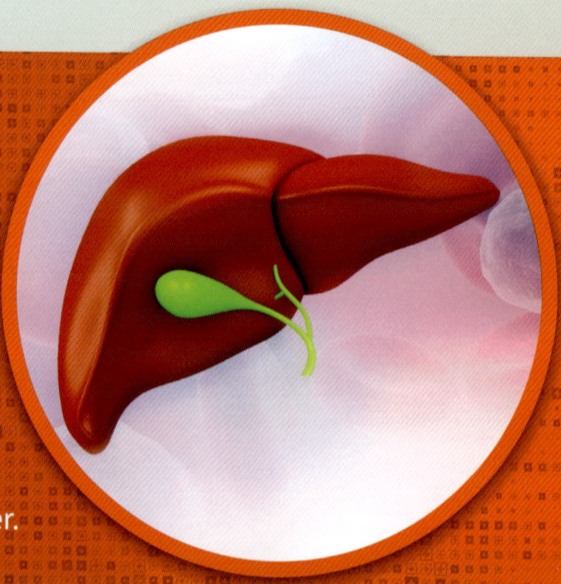

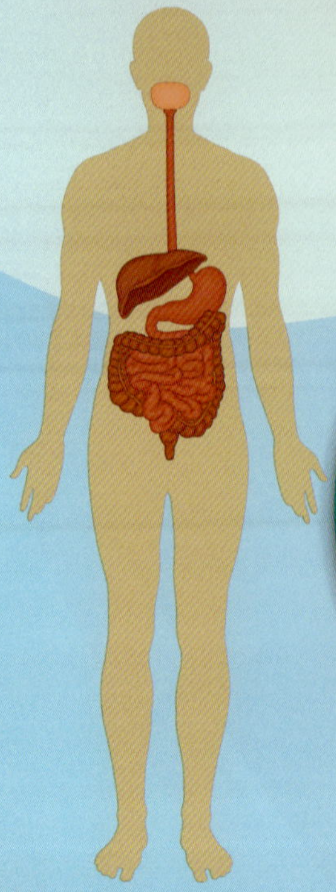

Storing Bile

Between meals, the gallbladder acts as a **reservoir** for bile. Storing bile is useful because it allows the body to release a large amount of the fluid quickly when fatty food enters the digestive tract. This allows the body to digest large quantities of fats when needed. Without the gallbladder, bile would only be able to trickle slowly into the intestine as the liver produced it, making fat digestion less efficient.

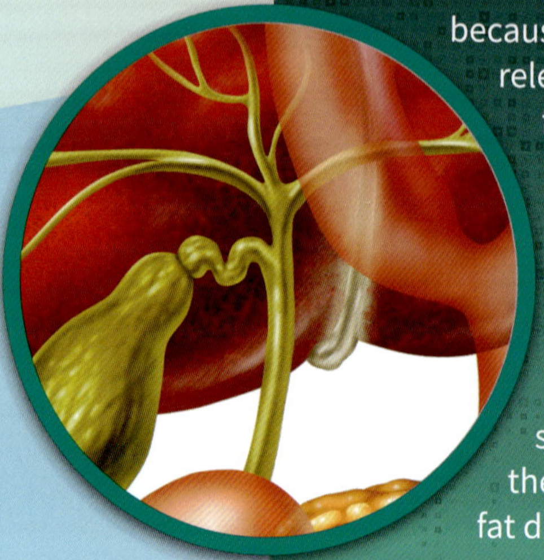

Compressing Bile

When bile is first made by the liver, it is about 95 percent water. However, when bile is stored in the gallbladder, most of this water is absorbed into the blood. This makes the bile more concentrated. Since concentrated bile contains a higher percentage of bile salts, it is more effective at digesting fats.

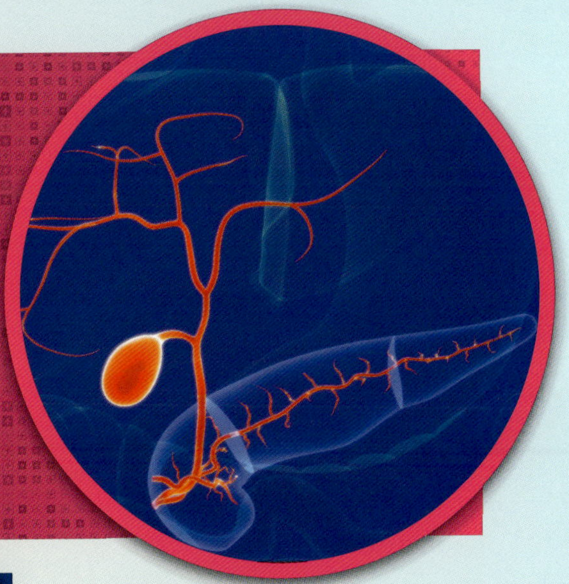

Releasing Bile

When the small intestine releases CCK, the muscles in the gallbladder squeeze. This pushes bile out through the cystic duct and into the common bile duct. Once bile enters the small intestine through a structure called the ampulla of Vater, the bile salts help break fats into smaller droplets. This process, called emulsification, makes it easier for digestive enzymes to finish breaking fats down into fatty acids, which the body is able to absorb.

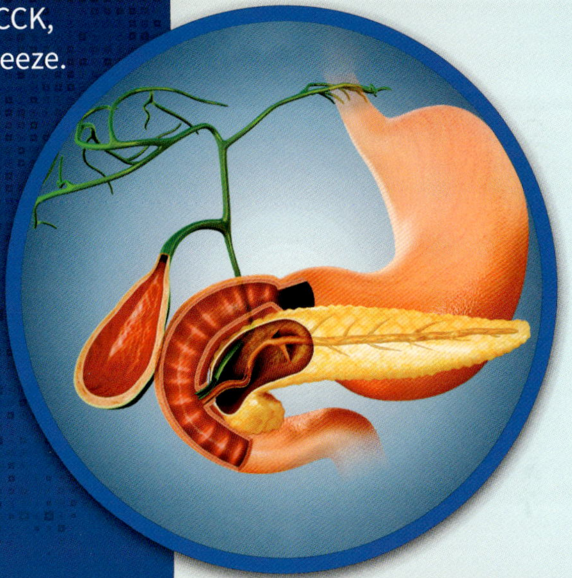

Can You Live Without It? YES!

The gallbladder is not one of the body's five vital organs, which means it is not essential for survival. If it becomes diseased or causes problems, it can be removed through a surgical procedure called a cholecystectomy. Without a gallbladder, the liver still produces bile, but there is no place to store and concentrate it. Bile flows continuously into the small intestine instead of being released when needed. Many people live healthy lives without a gallbladder. However, they may need to avoid eating large amounts of fatty foods at once.

A Medical Timeline

Coming from the Old English words *galla*, or "bile," and *blædre*, or "sac," the word *gallbladder* means "bile sac." This organ has been studied for centuries as part of the digestive system. Understanding its structure and function has helped doctors diagnose and treat many conditions.

circa 2000 BC

Clay models of the liver and gallbladder are sculpted in the ancient civilizations of Babylon and Assyria.

circa 1500 BC

An **ancient Egyptian** princess is preserved and buried as a mummy. Her gallbladder, which contains **gallstones**, stays intact for thousands of years and becomes the earliest example of gallstones to be found.

circa 300 BC

Doctors in India identify bile as one of the body's key fluids. They connect it to digestion and the **breakdown of food**.

1733 AD

French surgeon **Jean-Louis Petit** suggests the possibility of surgically removing gallstones by cutting into the organ.

1882

The first successful cholecystectomy is performed by German surgeon **Carl Langenbuch**. The patient recovers fully, proving that people can live without the gallbladder.

1892

Scottish surgeon **John Thomson** publishes his research on biliary atresia. This is a rare condition in which babies are born with blocked bile ducts.

1985

In Germany, Erich Mühe performs the first **laparoscopic cholecystectomy**. Recovery from a laparoscopic procedure is faster and less painful than traditional surgery.

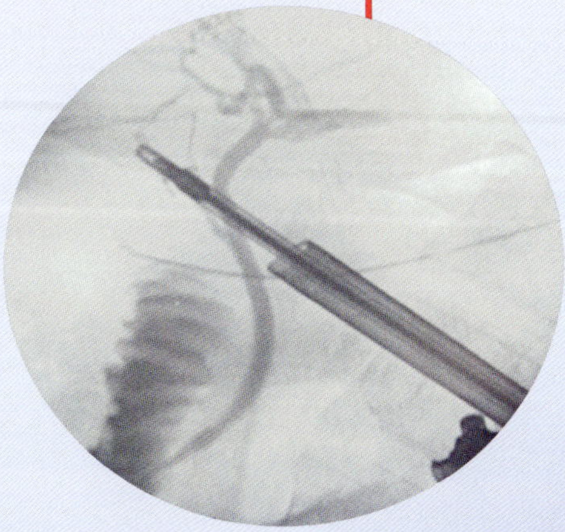

1988

The laparoscopic cholecystectomy procedure is introduced in the **United States**.

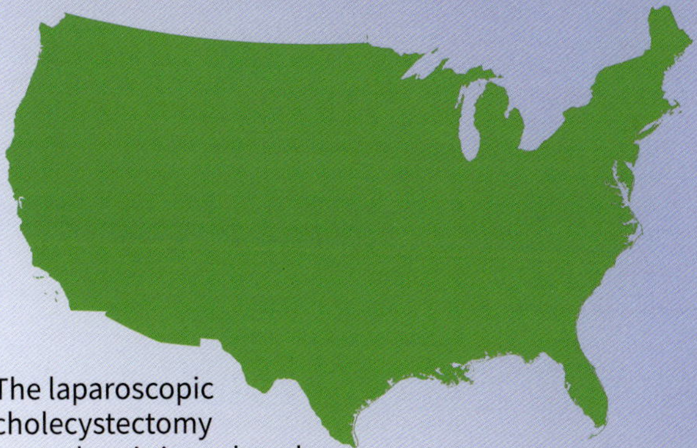

2019

Researchers develop **improved imaging methods** to observe the movement of bile through the biliary tree.

2025

Scientists use **artificial intelligence** (AI) to help analyze medical imaging and improve early detection of gallbladder diseases.

Organs Working Together

The fluids released by the biliary tree organs support the digestion that takes place in the organs of the GI tract. Bile released by the gallbladder aids in mechanical digestion, which involves physically breaking up food. Enzymes from the pancreas speed up **chemical digestion**.

The Gallbladder works with the...

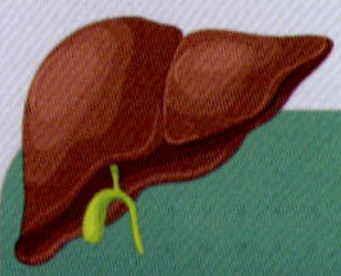

Liver, which Produces Bile and Removes Toxins

Liver breaks down old red blood cells → **Hemoglobin** is separated into parts, including heme, which contains iron → Heme is turned into biliverdin, a greenish bile pigment → Bilverdin becomes a yellowish bile pigment called bilirubin

Liver produces cholesterol and receives more from food → Hepatocytes convert cholesterol into bile acids → Bile acids are combined with **amino acids** to form bile salts → Bile salts are added to bile

Blood carries toxins to liver → Liver filters toxins, turning some into less harmful substances → Some toxins are sent to kidneys for removal in urine → Some toxins are added to bile and sent to gallbladder

Pancreas, which Releases Digestive Enzymes

Food enters small intestine from stomach through duodenum → Duodenum releases CCK if fats and proteins are present → CCK signals pancreas to release digestive enzymes, including lipases, amylases, and proteases → Digestive enzymes travel through pancreatic duct to duodenum

Lipase breaks down... Fats → Fatty acids and glycerol

Amylase breaks down... Carbohydrates → Glucose

Protease breaks down... Proteins → Amino acids

Small Intestine, which Receives Bile and Absorbs Nutrients

Food from stomach enters duodenum of small intestine → Duodenum releases CCK if fats and proteins are present → CCK signals gallbladder to contract and release bile → Bile travels through bile ducts to duodenum

Bile salts in bile surround fat droplets in food → Fats are emulsified into smaller particles → Emulsified fats are easier for lipases to break down → Small intestine is able to absorb fatty acids and glycerol

Diseases of the Gallbladder

Gallbladder problems typically affect the flow of bile. They can cause pain, infection, and other complications. Gallbladder conditions include gallstones, cholecystitis, biliary dyskinesia, and gallbladder cancer.

Gallstones

Gallstones form from cholesterol, bile pigments, or other substances found in bile. They may occur when bile is too concentrated and hardens as a result. Gallstones can be as small as a grain of sand or as large as a golf ball. Some people with gallstones, especially small ones, have no symptoms. Others experience pain, nausea, or digestive problems. Gallstones can block the flow of bile and lead to **inflammation** or infection.

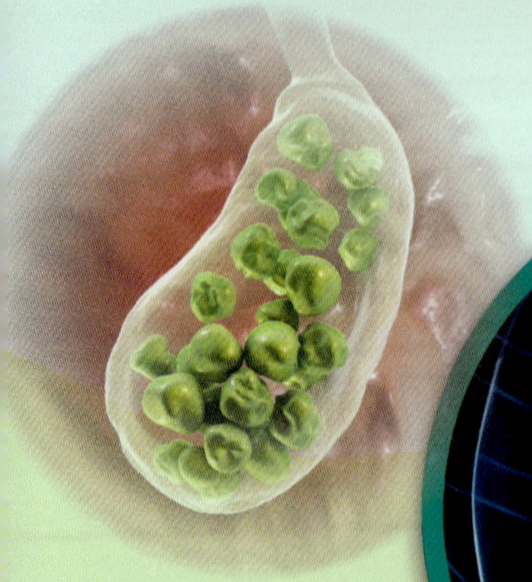

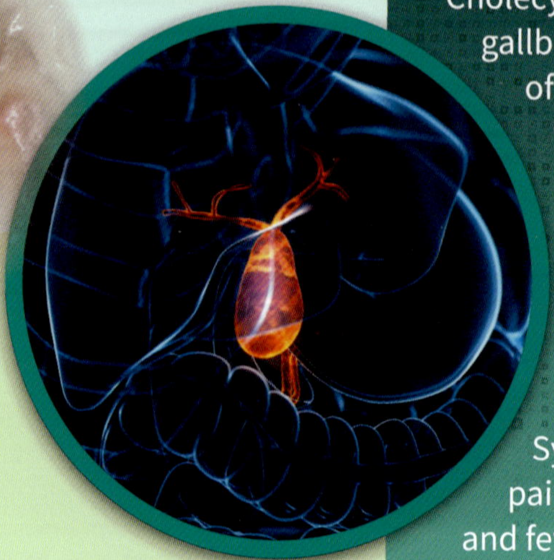

Cholecystitis

Cholecystitis is the inflammation of the gallbladder. It occurs when the flow of bile is obstructed, causing bile to build up in the gallbladder. Gallstones are the most common cause of cholecystitis. When they become lodged in bile ducts or the opening to the gallbladder, they block the flow of bile and sometimes lead to infections. Symptoms of cholecystitis include pain in the upper abdomen, nausea, and fever.

Biliary Dyskinesia

Biliary dyskinesia is a condition where the gallbladder does not empty properly. It is not able to fully contract and release bile into the bile ducts. This causes a buildup of bile in the gallbladder and decreases bile secretion into the small intestine, affecting the organ's ability to digest fatty foods. Pain in the upper abdomen, nausea, weight loss, and a bloated stomach are some possible symptoms.

Gallbladder Cancer

Cancer is a disease in which cells reproduce and spread uncontrollably. Gallbladder cancer is rare but serious. It begins in the cells lining the inside of the gallbladder. Symptoms may include abdominal pain, weight loss, nausea, or **jaundice**. Gallstones and cholecystitis can increase the risk of gallbladder cancer.

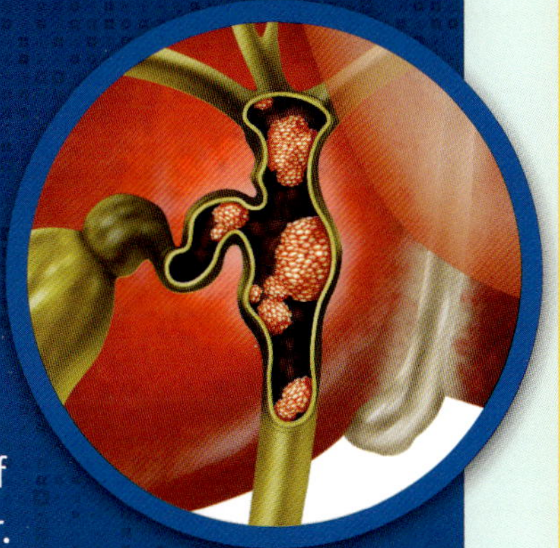

Warning Signs!

Gallbladder problems can develop into serious conditions. There are some symptoms to watch out for. If these signs appear, it is important to see a doctor.

- Pain in upper abdomen
- Pain after eating fatty foods
- Jaundice
- Frequent nausea and vomiting
- High fever with chills
- Pale stool
- Brown or dark urine

Progression of Gallstones

Most people with gallstones do not develop any symptoms. They have gallstones known as "silent stones." However, gallstones can sometimes progress into other conditions. In fact, most gallbladder diseases are caused by gallstones. Gallstones can also cause pancreatitis, or swelling and inflammation of the pancreas.

Gallstones → Blocked Bile Duct → Cholecystitis

Gallstones → Blocked Pancreatic Duct → Pancreatitis

Medicine around the World

The branch of medicine that treats the organs of the digestive system is called gastroenterology. Hospitals and universities around the world study the gallbladder to understand how it works and how to treat diseases that affect it. These centers also train doctors to perform surgeries and treat gallbladder diseases using the latest medical tools.

Johns Hopkins University, United States

1

Johns Hopkins University, in Baltimore, Maryland, is one of the leading hospitals in the United States for digestive disease care. Its surgeons perform a large number of laparoscopic cholecystectomies and other gallbladder procedures. Researchers at Johns Hopkins have also developed SRT-H, an advanced surgical robot that was able successfully remove the gallbladder from a **dummy** in 2025.

Norfolk and Norwich University Hospital, United Kingdom

2

Norfolk and Norwich University Hospital (NNUH) is a large teaching hospital that trains hundreds of medical students. It works closely with the nearby Quadram Institute, which houses one of the largest **endoscopy** centers in Europe. The Quadram Institute performs more than 40,000 endoscopies each year. Many of these are used to detect gallstones and other problems affecting the biliary tree. Patients are then treated as needed by NNUH's gastroenterology department.

King Fahad Medical City, Saudi Arabia

3

King Fahad Medical City is located in Riyadh, Saudi Arabia's capital city. Doctors in its gastroenterology department use imaging methods such as ultrasounds, magnetic resonance imaging (MRIs), and endoscopy to examine the gallbladder and bile ducts. The hospital also treats children with biliary atresia and works to reduce complications by detecting the disease early.

Singapore General Hospital, Singapore

4

Singapore General Hospital is the oldest and largest hospital in Singapore. Its Department of Hepatopancreatobiliary (HPB) and Transplant Surgery performs complex procedures on the organs and ducts of the biliary tree. The hospital uses advanced imaging methods to detect gallstones and performs **minimally invasive** surgery to remove them if needed.

What is a Gastroenterologist?

A gastroenterologist is a doctor who specializes in diagnosing and treating diseases of the digestive system. Tools such as endoscopes and ultrasounds help gastroenterologists examine the inside of the body. Some gastroenterologists further specialize in treating the liver, pancreas, gallbladder, and bile ducts. These specialists are called hepatologists. They treat gallstones, bile duct blockages, and other biliary tree conditions.

Keeping the Gallbladder Healthy

A healthy gallbladder supports overall digestion. Practice habits that keep the gallbladder and bile ducts working properly. Eating the right foods and staying active may help prevent problems such as gallstones.

TIP 1

Stay Hydrated

Drinking plenty of water prevents bile from becoming too concentrated. This reduces the risk of gallstones. Aim to drink at least eight glasses of water each day.

TIP 2

Eat Foods High in Fiber

Fiber helps move food through the digestive system. Eating fruits and vegetables, which are high in both fiber and water, improves digestive health.

TIP 3

Reduce Unhealthy Fats

Reduce or avoid greasy and fried foods. These are high in unhealthy fats that can lead to gallstones.

TIP 4

Stay Active

Exercise helps control weight and improves digestion. Aim for at least 30 minutes of physical activity each day.

TIP 5

Eat Regular Meals

Skipping meals or fasting for long periods can cause bile to build up and form gallstones. Eating regular, balanced meals keeps bile flowing and helps the gallbladder empty frequently.

Activity: Emulsification with Soap

Bile salts act as emulsifiers, surrounding large **globules** of fats to break them into smaller droplets. Soap is another example of an emulsifier. Try this activity with soap, oil, and water to gain a better understanding of how bile works to separate fats.

Materials

- Clear cup or glass
- Water
- Cooking oil
- Dish soap
- Spoon
- Pen and paper

Steps

1. **Prepare the Mixture:** Fill the glass halfway with water. Then, add a spoonful of oil, which is a type of fat. Watch what happens. The oil should float on top of the water.

2. **Stir the Mixture:** Try stirring the mixture with the spoon. This represents the muscles in the digestive system that churn and mix food. Observe whether the oil mixes with the water. You will notice that the oil and water continue to form separate layers.

3. **Add the Dish Soap:** Add a few drops of dish soap to the cup. The soap represents bile. Stir the mixture gently with the spoon.

4. **Observe the Changes:** Watch how the oil changes. The soap breaks the oil into smaller droplets that spread through the water. This is similar to how bile breaks down fat in the small intestine.

5. **Try More Tests:** What happens if you do not stir the mixture? What about if you add more dish soap? Try some variations of the experiment and record your observations.

6. **Analyze and Discuss:** Compare what happened with and without the dish soap. How did the soap help the oil mix with water? What does this explain about bile's role in digestion? Write down your conclusions.

Quiz

1

Which organ produces bile?

2

Who performed the first successful cholecystectomy?

3

What are gallstones composed of?

4

What is another name for the gallbladder?

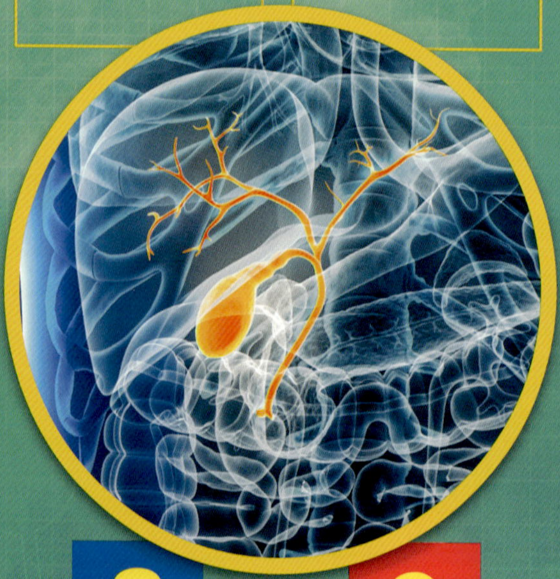

5

Which component of bile breaks down fats?

6

Is the gallbladder part of the GI tract?

7

What is cholecystitis?

8

Which biological molecules does amylase help the body digest?

9

What does the word *gallbladder* mean?

10

Which hormone signals the gallbladder to contract?

ANSWERS

1. Liver **2.** German surgeon Carl Langenbuch **3.** Cholesterol, bile pigments, or other substances found in bile **4.** Cholecyst **5.** Bile salts **6.** No **7.** Inflammation of the gallbladder **8.** Carbohydrates **9.** "Bile sac" **10.** Cholecystokinin (CCK)

Key Words

abdominal cavity: the hollow space in the body that holds organs such as the stomach, liver, gallbladder, and intestines

amino acids: molecules that combine to form proteins

cells: the basic units of all living organisms

chemical digestion: the process that changes the structure of food molecules into forms that the body is able to absorb

concentrates: makes a liquid thicker and stronger by removing water from it

digestive: relating to the process of breaking down food into forms that the body can absorb

dummy: a model of a human or body part that is used for medical training

endoscopy: medical procedure that uses a thin tube to look inside the body

enzymes: specialized proteins that speed up chemical reactions

gallstones: hardened pieces of bile that form inside the gallbladder

globules: round drops, especially of fat or a liquid

hemoglobin: a protein in red blood cells that carries oxygen around the body

hepatic: relating to the liver

homeostasis: the body's ability to maintain a stable internal environment despite external changes

hormones: chemical messengers that affect many functions in the body

inflammation: the body's response to injury or infection, often resulting in redness, swelling, heat, or pain

jaundice: a yellowing of the skin and eyes caused by too much bilirubin in the blood

minimally invasive: relating to surgical procedures that use smaller cuts than open surgery, reducing pain and recovery time

molecules: the smallest unit of a substance

nutrients: substances in food that the body uses for energy, growth, and repair

organ: a distinct structure in the body that is made up of tissues and performs one or more specific functions

pathogens: microorganisms, such as bacteria or viruses, that cause diseases

pigments: substances that give color to things

reservoir: a place that stores a fluid for later use

smooth muscle: muscle tissue that works automatically without conscious control

Index

LIGHTBOX

SUPPLEMENTARY RESOURCES

Click on the plus icon found in the bottom left corner of each spread to open additional teacher resources.

- Download and print the book's quizzes and activities
- Access curriculum correlations
- Explore additional web applications that enhance the Lightbox experience

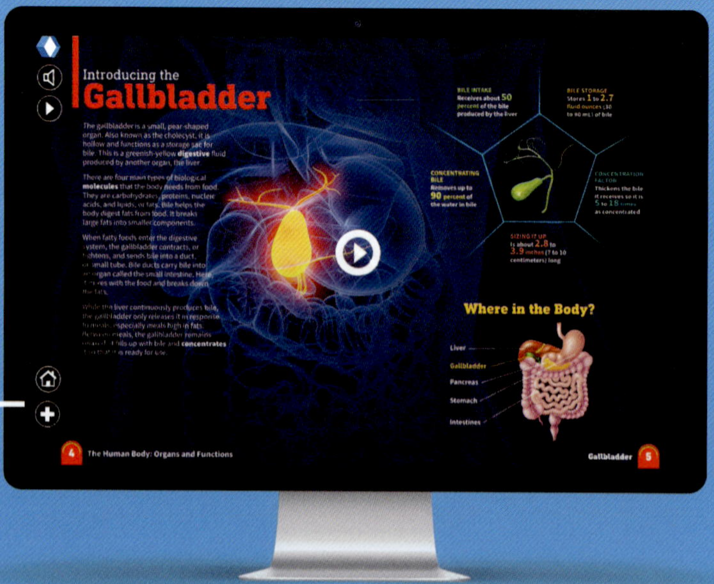

LIGHTBOX DIGITAL TITLES

Packed full of integrated media

VIDEOS

INTERACTIVE MAPS

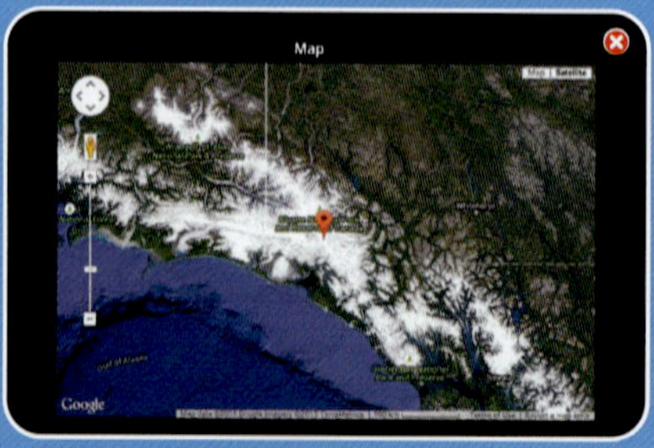

WEBLINKS

SLIDESHOWS

QUIZZES

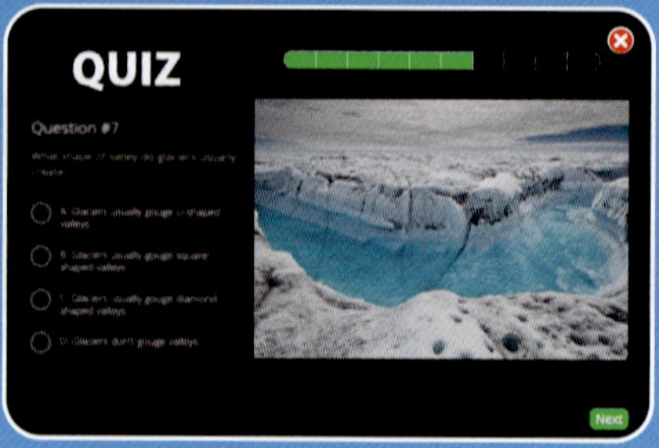

OPTIMIZED FOR

- ✓ TABLETS
- ✓ SMART BOARDS
- ✓ COMPUTERS
- ✓ AND MUCH MORE!

Published by Lightbox Learning Inc.
276 5th Avenue, Suite 704 #917
New York, NY 10001
Website: www.openlightbox.com

Library of Congress Control Number: 2025932683

ISBN 978-1-5105-8693-2 (hardcover)
ISBN 978-1-5105-8694-9 (static multi-user eBook)
ISBN 978-1-5105-8696-3 (interactive multi-user eBook)

Printed in Fargo, North Dakota, in the United States of America
1 2 3 4 5 6 7 8 9 0 29 28 27 26 25

082025
111024

Project Coordinator: Priyanka Das
Design: Jean Faye Rodriguez